Introduction

Welcome to Lean Rhino's Food Safety Leaders Training! We are very glad that you are investing the time and effort to go through this course.

Our goal is to:

- Provide you with excellent and accurate food safety information
- Give you the tools to take with you to the workplace
- Get you certified in food safety

When you complete this course, you will be given the option to take an exam.

Taking and passing the exam with a minimum 70% is required for government certification.

TABLE OF CONTENTS

Module [1]

Food Safety In Canada

The goal of this section is to help you understand the role that different government agencies have with Food Safety in Canada.

Food Safety in Canada

 Goal

The goal of this section is to help you understand the role that different government agencies have with Food Safety in Canada.

Things to Remember

The food industry is governed by several levels of government in Canada.
- Local or Regional
- Provincial
- Federal

Owners/managers of food operations are required to follow all the Food Safety Regulations that applies to them.

Owners/managers of food operations are responsible for the safety of the food they produce.

Food Safety Facts

Although Canada enjoys a very good food safety system, there is still the need for improvement.

According to the Conference Board of Canada, there are approximately 6.8 Million cases of foodborne illness each year.

- According to the conference board of Canada almost 70 per cent of these illnesses are acquired outside the home such as from restaurants, catering facilities etc.

Food-borne illness is still happening and needs to be controlled!

Food Borne Illness - why is this important?

Most foodborne illness infections can be managed but some illnesses may result in long term health damage and even cause death.

"High Risk Populations" are those individuals that can be severely affected or die from foodborne illnesses.

Some of these groups of individuals or High-Risk Populations are:

- Young children
- Children and/or Adults with an immune compromising disease
- Pregnant women
- Elder population

Food Safety Regulations

There are several levels of government that regulate food safety in Canada:

- Federal Government
- Provincial Government
- Regional Health Authorities

Federal Government   manipatore

The Canadian Food Inspection Agency and Health Canada are responsible for food safety at the federal level.

The Canadian Food Inspection Agency works to enforce the Food and Drugs act as well as other food safety policies and standards, set by Health Canada, ensuring the safety and nutritional quality of food sold in Canada.

Food products such as meat, dairy, poultry and honey that cross provincial or international borders are inspected and regulated by the Canadian Food Inspection Agency (CFIA). CFIA employ food safety specialists to inspect federally registered food facilities and make sure they meet the requirements of the federal Regulations.

Health Canada is the research and policy development agency. They conduct research and determine the appropriate policies needed to ensure food safety in Canada.

Provincial Government

Each province and territory in Canada has provincial food safety regulations. For example:

- Alberta – Public Health Act and the Food Regulation

- British Columbia – Public Health Act and the Food Premises Regulation
- Saskatchewan – The Public Health Act and the Food Safety Regulations

These Regulations are developed provincially by agencies such as Alberta Health in Alberta, Ministry of Health in British Columbia and Saskatchewan Ministry of Health. These agencies will develop food safety laws that are then enforced by the Regional Health Authorities.

Regional Health Authorities

Within each province there are regional health authorities that are mandated to enforce food safety Regulations. With the exception of Alberta where there is only one Regional Health Authority, Alberta Health Services, other provinces will have multiple health authorities responsible for geographic areas of the province.

These Regional Health Authorities employ health inspectors who conduct inspections of food businesses to ensure they are meeting the requirements of the food safety regulations. They are responsible for:

- Ensure compliance with Food Safety Regulations
- Take action when the public health is at risk
- Provide expert knowledge on food safety

Health Inspectors are a fantastic resource for food business owners and employees. They are a wealth of information and are willing to support food safety improvements.

Here are some helpful hints for when an inspector is conducting an inspection at your facility:

- Follow the health inspector during the inspection
- Demonstrate to the inspector food safety controls you have in place
- Ask the inspector to clarify inspection reports and be sure to understand the Regulations for your province.

Do your part for Safe Food:

- ☐ Understand and follow your local food safety Regulations.
- ☐ Keep your food safety knowledge up to date by engaging in continuous learning.
- ☐ Implement a food safety management system
- ☐ Become a food safety champion

Module 2

Facility Design

The goal of this section is to understand the important role that facility design and construction has on food safety.

Facility Design

1 Goal

The goal of this section is to understand the important role that facility design and construction has on food safety.

Things to Remember

Proper design and flow of the food facility will help prevent contamination of food products and equipment.

For example, if the receiving of packaged goods is in the same area as food preparation, there is a higher chance that packaging materials, blood juices from raw meats, and dirt will end up on food contact surfaces and contaminate the food.

Important Messages on Facility Construction:

Location:
- A food facility should not be located near chemical plants, landfills, or livestock operations.

Flow:
- Proper flow of food and staff will reduce the possibility of food and equipment contamination.

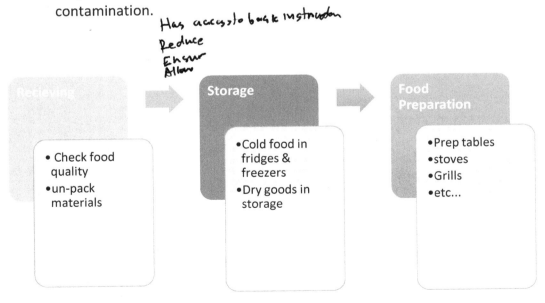

Floors:
- Made of smooth, durable and easy to clean material
- Joints are sealed to baseboards
- Sloped towards a drain for easy cleaning

Walls and Ceilings:
- Made of smooth, durable and easy to clean materials

Lighting:
- Strong enough to allow for proper cleaning and sanitation.

Ventilation:
- Adequate to remove cooking grease vapors
- Cleaned often to prevent the risk of fire

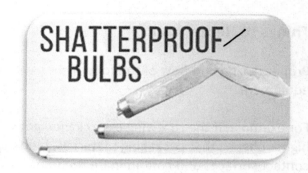

Washroom facilities:
- Do not open on food preparation areas
- Clean and stocked with soap, warm running water and paper towels to promote hand-washing.

Potable Water:
- "Potable Water" means water that is safe for human consumption.
- Water supply must be approved by Health Authority.
  - Municipal / city water supply is usually safe.
  - Private water supply such as wells, need to be approved and regularly tested.

Hand washing facilities:
- Food preparation areas must be equipped with a designated (designated means it cannot be used for anything else except for washing hands) hand washing station
- Hand washing station must be equipped with soap, paper towel or hand dryer, hot and cold running water and a garbage bin.

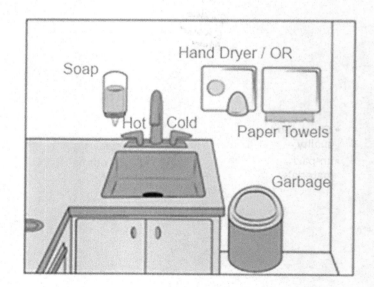

Food contact surfaces:

- Food contact surfaces have to be smooth, durable and easy to clean
- They have to be non-corrosive, non-absorbent, non-toxic, and free from cracks, crevices, or pitting.
- The "Reference Listing of Accepted Construction, Packaging and Non-Food Chemical Agents", published by Canadian Food Inspection Agency (CFIA) outlines coatings, chemicals, lubricants and other acceptable material for food contact surfaces.

Safe food practices:

- Check with construction engineers and plumbers that there is no piping cross-connections or backflow potential on your water supply.
- Routine maintenance of food facility should be done regularly by qualified workers.

Proper food facility design will:

- Reduce the risk of cross-contamination of food
- Ensure food contact surfaces are easily cleanable
- Allow for food safety controls such as proper storage of food and non-food items.

Your notes:

About Equipment

Equipment design and construction can play a vital role in the sanitation and safety of the food production in a food facility.

There are a number of standards and agencies that approve equipment for use in food service/food manufacturing facilities. Here are some equipment certification agencies commonly used to certify food equipment:

- National Sanitation Foundation (NSF): The NSF's main focus is certifying products (equipment used in food facilities as an example) as having been tested and audited to meet safety standards.
- Underwriters Laboratories (UL): The UL agency certifies the design and safety of electrical and gas fired food service equipment among others.
- Canadian Standards Association (CSA): CSA also tests and certifies electrical and gas equipment.

Although the NSF, UL, and CSA are fairly common certifying agencies, there are other agencies that develop standards and certify food equipment. It is crucial to ensure food equipment is certified, inspected and approved before using it to produce food.

Your notes:

Starting a Food Business in Alberta

 2 **Goal**

To understand the process for starting a food business in Alberta.

Things to Remember

- ✍ In Alberta, food safety is governed by the Alberta Food Regulation (Alberta Regulation 31/2006)
- ✍ There is only one Health Region in Alberta and there are a number of Environmental Health Offices across the province
- ✍ Anyone operating a food business **must** have a valid Food Handling Permit from Alberta Health Services
- ✍ The Food Handling Permit is <u>only valid for one year and must renewed each year</u>
- ✍ The Food Handling Permit is not transferable, meaning if you sell or buy an existing business you must apply for a separate Food Handling Permit
- ✍ All Food Handling Permits must be posted in a **visible** place for the public to see.

Process for Starting a Food Business in Alberta

Step #1: **Municipal Requirements**

The local city or Municipal District has zoning and business license requirements that must be met. For example, occupancy requirements, fire code, building code etc. The first step is to contact your local municipality and follow their process for gaining a business license and occupancy approval.

Step #2: **Develop and submit your plans**

Construction and/or renovation plans must meet local building codes and health requirements. It is recommended that you work with contractors that have similar

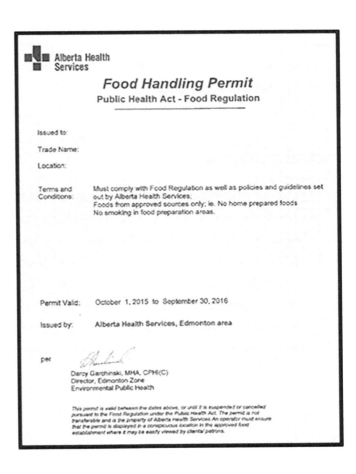

previous experience as well as ensure an Environmental Health Officer has approved the plan prior to beginning construction.

Step #3: **Register in Food Safety Training and Begin Construction**

The Alberta Food Regulation (Section 31) requires food handlers to have approved food safety training certificates. The requirements for training are:

- At least one person trained in food safety where there are 5 or fewer food handlers (this typically includes wait staff). The trained individual does not have to be present at all times. Of course, other staff members have to still understand food safety requirements and are responsible to handle food safely.
- Where there are 6 or more staff, there has to be someone on-site at all times that has the food safety training certificate.

Step #4: **Complete construction and get occupancy permit**

Once the construction is completed, municipal codes officers can approve the building and provide building and occupancy permit.

Step #5: **Get Health Inspection and pay for your food handling permit**

Health Inspectors will then be able to approve the food handling permit. There is a fee for the Food Handling Permit, so once the fee is paid and the premises is approved you can begin operating your food business.

Starting a Food Business from Home

- ✒ Using a home kitchen to operate a food business from home is not allowed
- ✒ The only exception is at approved Farmers Markets. Farmers Markets approved by Alberta Agriculture allow individuals to prepare food at home and sell to the public.
- ✒ A home-based food business can be allowed if a portion of your home is constructed and designed to meet the requirements of the Food Regulation. Using your regular home kitchen does not meet this requirement as it has to be a separate kitchen.
- ✒ A home-based food business will also need a Food Handling Permit and will go through a similar process as the one mentioned above.

Module 3

Biological, Chemical Physical Hazards

The goal of this section is to help you understand the different hazards that can contaminate food and how to control them.

Micro-organisms

 Goal

The goal of this section is to help you understand the different types and characteristics of micro-organisms and how they grow, spread and cause foodborne illness.

Things to Remember

- A micro-organism is a tiny organism (micro part of the word).
- Not all micro-organisms are harmful
- Micro-organisms are so small they cannot be seen without the use of a microscope.

Micro-organisms can be:

Inert - neither beneficial nor harmful for humans.
There are micro-organisms that do not hurt or help humans in any way. Since inert organisms do not harm or help humans, we don't worry about them here.

Beneficial - interact in a positive way with humans and the food they consume.
These organisms have a positive influence on food production. For example, consider yeast and its role in making bread. Another example is the bacterial cultures that help with the production of cheeses and other dairy products. Those are all considered beneficial micro-organisms.

Spoilage - damage or spoil the quality of the food but are NOT harmful.
We've all seen mouldy bread, or wilted lettuce. This spoilage is caused by the spoilage micro-organisms. For the most part these organisms do not cause harm to humans, but do cause damage to food products.

Pathogenic - harmful for human beings.
This is the class of micro-organisms that causes foodborne illness in humans. Since our goal is safe food preparation is to stop these types of organisms from growing, we will focus mostly on this group in this course.

> A **pathogen** is defined as a disease-causing micro-organism.

Biological Hazards

 Goal

The goal of this section is to help you understand the different **biological hazards** that can contaminate food and how to control them

Things to Remember

A Hazard is a danger or risk! There are four main categories of hazards for people from food:

1. Biological
2. Chemical
3. Physical
4. Allergies

Biological Hazards

Biological hazards occur when harmful micro-organisms contaminate food directly or by cross-contamination.

Cross-contamination – is the indirect contamination of food by contaminated food contact surfaces, other food ingredients and/or equipment.

Micro-organisms can be grouped as:

- Bacteria ╱
- Viruses ╱
- Parasites ╱╔ᴷⁱˡˡˢ
- Fungi ╱

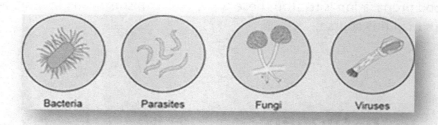

Bacteria

Bacteria are found everywhere. Most are harmless, but there are a few pathogenic types that make up the majority of food borne illnesses.

If the conditions are right, bacteria can <u>multiply very quickly</u>.

For example, under the right conditions, bacteria can double in numbers every 10 – 20 minutes.

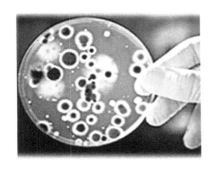

That means that only a handful of bacteria can become millions in just a few hours!

| 0 min | 20 min | 40 min | 60 min | 80 min | 10 hours |
| 1 bacteria | 2 bacteria | 4 bacteria | 8 bacteria | 16 bacteria | Over 1 billion bacteria |

Bacteria need FATTOM to grow:

F-   Food
A-   Acidity
T-   Time
T-   Temperature
O-   Oxygen
M-   Moisture

F – Food

- Just like humans, bacteria need food to grow.
- Proteins such as meat, poultry, and seafood have ideal nutrients for bacteria to grow.

A – Acidity

- The pH scale measures the acidity of food.
- The scale goes from 1 – 14 with the smaller the number the more acidic the food will be, 7 being neutral and the higher numbers being alkaline.
- Most pathogenic bacteria have a preference of pH ranging from 4.6 – 7.
- Chicken, and eggs for example fall under this pH range.

T – Temperature

- Most pathogenic bacteria prefer temperatures that are between 4°C (40°F) and 60°C (140°F).
- Keeping food in your refrigerator for example will keep it at or below 4°C (40°F) and will limit most pathogenic bacteria from growing.

T – Time

- Bacteria need time to grow.
- Bacteria can double in number every 20 minutes so 1 bacteria cell can become 64 in 2 hours. throw the food
- Considering some pathogenic (harmful) bacteria can cause illness with as little as 4 or 5 bacteria, it is important to limit the time that bacteria can grow.

O – Oxygen

0 to 1   of 0.86 or Higher

- Some bacteria need oxygen in order to grow – these are called Aerobic bacteria.
- Some bacteria can only grow in the absence of oxygen – these are called anaerobic bacteria.
- Some bacteria can grow in either oxygen or no oxygen environments – these are called facultative bacteria.

Aerobic	Needs Oxygen
Anaerobic	Absence of oxygen is needed
Facultative	Can grow with or without oxygen

Modified Atmospheric Packaging (MAP)
Since most spoilage bacteria need oxygen to grow, modified atmospheric packaging is a process of extending shelf life of products by removing oxygen and replacing it with a gas mixture (normally Co_2 and N_2). This process can also be called "reduced oxygen packaging".

Although there are many benefits to MAP, there are also health risks if it is not done properly.

M – Moisture (water)

- Bacteria can grow best in food items that have high moisture or available water.
- Available water is measured in aw on a scale of 0 to 1.
- Most high moisture food items have available water (aw) of 0.86 or higher.
- This is why drying food items can lower the chances of bacteria from growing e.g. beef jerky.

Perishable, Potentially Hazardous and Non-Hazardous Foods

Cook Carbohydrates

Things to Remember

Perishable food products - are those most likely to "spoil".

Examples of Perishable Food Products

- ✓ Dairy products such as milk and yoghurt. Both milk and yoghurt will spoil if not consumed within a few days.
- ✓ Fruits and Vegetables such as lettuce tomatoes and avocados. For example, lettuce left in the refrigerator for too long will wilt and spoil.
- ✓ Raw meat is another example of a food product that will spoil if not consumed within a few days.

One way to know if a product is perishable is to look for a "best before date". These dates are often listed to ensure the product is consumed before it spoils.

In contrast an "expiry date" is often a date set whereby after that date, the food may not be safe to eat.

Potentially Hazardous Food Products

A potentially hazardous food is any food product that has the potential to allow growth of harmful microbes and the formation of toxins in the food. If Potentially Hazardous food products are not handled safely they can support the growth of pathogenic bacteria such as Salmonella which cause foodborne illness.

A food is considered potentially hazardous if:

- Can support the growth of pathogenic bacteria – often has protein (or the Food component needed for organisms to grow).
- Has a pH greater than 4.6

  Or

- Has water activity greater than 0.85

Examples of Potentially Hazardous Food Products

- Foods that contain dairy products such as cheese, milk, custards etc.
- Raw and cooked meat products such as hamburgers, meat pies, curries, etc.
- Raw and cooked seafood such as sushi, lobster, fish etc.
- Fruits and Vegetables
- Cooked carbohydrates such as pastas, rice, etc.
- Sandwiches that contain meat, cheese, or vegetable ingredients are also considered perishable

Any dry food such as beans, rice, lentils, etc. becomes **perishable** with cooking and/or the addition of **moisture/water**.

Why is this important?

Foodborne illness infections can be caused by mishandling of potentially hazardous food products. It's important to understand how to identify potentially hazardous food products in order to control pathogenic bacteria growth.

Non-Hazardous Foods are products that do not support the growth of pathogenic micro-organisms

Examples of Non-Hazardous Food Products

- Dry rice,
- Uncooked pasta,
- High acidic foods such as sauerkraut, pickles, etc.

Do your part for Safe Food:
- ☐ Learn to recognize potentially hazardous foods
- ☐ Handle potentially hazardous food products safely

Your notes:

Common Foodborne Illness

There are three types of foodborne illness:

- Infections
- Intoxications
- Toxin infections

> **Incubation Period** is the time from when a person is infected with a pathogen i.e. consumes contaminated food to the time illness symptoms appear.

Foodborne Infections

- This happens when harmful bacteria are consumed and the bacteria causes the foodborne illness.
- The infection typically occurs 12 – 48 hours after consuming the contaminated food. This is the "incubation period".

Foodborne Intoxications

- This happens when the food is contaminated with toxins produced by bacteria and the toxin causes the foodborne illness.
- An example of this is Staphylococcus aureus bacteria.
- This bacterium grows on sores, boils on the skin and pimples. The bacteria get in the food and if allowed to grow, it produces toxins which cause the illness.

Foodborne Toxin Infections

- This happens when a pathogen that is consumed is also a toxin producing bacteria.
- In this case, the bacteria AND the toxin it produces causes the illness.
- It is a combination of an infection and intoxication.
- Toxin infections can be quite serious and may lead to long term permanent health problems in infected individuals.

Common Foodborne Pathogens

Common Foodborne Pathogen	Incubation Period	Symptoms	Commonly implicated Food Types
Bacteria			
Bacillus cereus	Toxin – 30min – 6 hours Infection – 6-15 hours	Nausea, vomiting, abdominal cramps, diarrhea	Cooked rice
Campylobacter	2-5 days	Diarrhea (sometimes bloody), Abdominal pain, headache, nausea, vomiting, fever	Poultry
Clostridium botulinum	18-36 hours (can be longer)	Weakness, vertigo, double vision, difficulty speaking & swallowing and other neurological symptoms	Home canned foods
Escherichia coli (E.coli)	2-9 days	Diarrhea (could be bloody), abdominal cramps, vomiting, occasional low grade fever. Can lead to Kidney failure (Hemolytic Uremic Syndrome or HUS)	Undercooked ground meat and other meat products
Listeria monocytogenes	Days to weeks	Nausea, vomiting, diarrhea, headache, fever. Can lead to meningitis	Processed meats, soft cheeses
Salmonella species	6-48 hours	Abdominal pain, headache, nausea, vomiting, fever, diarrhea	Meat, Poultry, Eggs, and Dairy
Shigella	12 – 50 hours	Diarrhea (sometimes bloody), Abdominal pain, headache, nausea, vomiting, fever,	Tuna and seafood salads, unpasteurized dairy products, poultry
Staphylococcus aureus	Few minutes (very quick onset of symptoms)	Nausea, vomiting, abdominal cramps	Ham, Poultry, Produce

Pathogenic Bacteria are also spread by humans contaminating food during food handling.

Viruses

- Do not multiply on food, but multiply inside the person and cause illness.
- Can live on surfaces, such as door knobs, for a long time.
- Most common food viruses are Norwalk like viruses, and Hepatitis A.

Common Foodborne Pathogen	Associated Food Types
Viruses	
Hepatitus A	Shellfish, raw fruit and vegetables
Norwalk agents	Shellfish

Parasites

- Live inside animals and humans.
- Can be spread by food such as raw fish and shellfish.
- Most common food parasite is Anisakis.

Common Foodborne Pathogen	Associated Food Types
Parasites	
Anisakiasis	Raw seafood in sushi products
Trichinella spiralis	Undercooked meat, pork

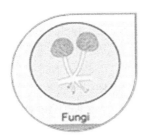

Fungi

- Includes moulds and yeasts
- Some moulds produce toxins that will make people sick.
- Foods with visible mould should be discarded.

Why is this important?

Controlling Biological hazards prevents foodborne illness.

Chemical Hazards

 Goal

The goal of this section is to help you understand the different **chemical hazards** that can contaminate food.

Things to Remember

A Chemical hazard is the potential for various chemicals in the food facility to contaminate the food and cause illness. Cleaning chemicals, equipment maintenance chemicals, pest control chemicals and even some food ingredients may contaminate food.

For example: Sodium Nitrite is a chemical used for the curing of meat. When used properly, it can prevent bacterial growth. However, adding too much Sodium Nitrite to meat can be toxic.

How to Control Chemical Hazards

	Agricultural chemicals	Sanitation Chemicals	Naturally Occurring Toxins	Toxic Metals
Chemical Type	• Pesticides • Antibiotics • Herbicides • Fertilizers	• Degreasers • Sanitizers • Non-food grade machine lubricants	• Seafood toxins • Moulds • Some plant toxins	• Metals used for utensils and pans • Metal storage containers
Control Steps	✓ Wash all produce thoroughly before using ✓ Buy food items only from government approved sources ✓ Ask if the supplier has a food safety program such as HACCP in their facility.	✓ Store all chemicals away from food areas in a closed and secure area ✓ Label all chemical bottles with the correct chemical ✓ Purchase food grade lubricants. ✓ Choose food safe approved suppliers for your sanitizing chemicals.	✓ Only purchase seafood from government approved food suppliers. ✓ You can always ask your supplier to prove their food handling permit to you before purchasing your food. ✓ Discard any food with visible mould growth.	✓ Purchase all your food utensils and equipment from reputable suppliers. ✓ Look for NSF certification. ✓ This will help you determine that the equipment was tested to be food-grade.

Physical Hazards

 Goal

The goal of this section is to help you understand how **physical hazards** can contaminate food.

Things to Remember

A physical hazard is the possibility that various objects or "foreign material" can end up in the food. Physical hazards can range from broken glass to peeling paint and can cause injury if not controlled.

How to Control Physical Hazards

- ☐ Are all your equipment/utensils in good physical condition? Examples:
    - ☐ No loose screws, nuts or bolts in any of the larger equipment
    - ☐ Cutting boards are smooth and not cracking or splintering (if they are wood)
    - ☐ Knives, scoops, and other utensils in good condition
- ☐ Are packaging materials disposed of immediately after removing food products from them?
- ☐ Are floors, walls, ceilings in good condition and there is no peeling paint
- ☐ Are staff members bringing equipment and other personal belongings into the food preparation and storage areas?
- ☐ Is maintenance equipment kept separate from food storage and preparation areas?
- ☐ Are external contractors (such as those cleaning and fixing equipment at the facility) cleaning up after they have completed the work and before food preparation begins?

Do your part for Safe Food:

- ☐ Dispose of broken or chipped equipment or utensils.
- ☐ Set and keep a regular equipment maintenance program for all equipment and facility.
- ☐ Keep food preparation and storage areas clean and free from un-used or unwanted things.

Your notes:

Case Study

One of the customers at the three hills restaurant, a 5-year-old child, began to choke on something in the food during the dinner service. The child was rushed to the hospital with bleeding in the throat. After undergoing surgery, the doctors removed a 3mm long piece of metal from the child's throat.

The health department later tracked the piece of metal to a broken and frayed strainer in the kitchen. Following this incident, the restaurant went out of business because of charges by the health department and a law suit filed by the child's parents.

How could this have been prevented?

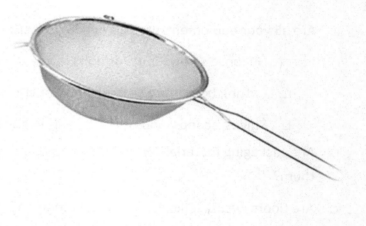

The restaurant owner, manager, and staff could have prevented this incident if they had been watching for physical contaminants. Then, they could have thrown away the broken strainer before it contaminated the child's food.

List some of the things you can do to prevent physical contamination:

Your notes:

Module 4

Purchase, Delivery, Storage

The goal of this section is to understand how sourcing ingredients from approved suppliers and ensuring they are transported safely and in sanitary conditions can prevent foodborne illness.

Purchasing and Receiving

 Goal

The goal of this section is to understand how sourcing ingredients from approved suppliers and ensuring they are transported safely and in sanitary conditions can prevent foodborne illness.

Things to Remember

Food can become contaminated if transported improperly and in unsanitary conditions. Contamination can be biological (pathogens), chemical, or physical materials.

Proper transportation of food such as safe storage in delivery trucks as well as proper temperature control can prevent food contamination.

Purchasing Food Products

Purchase all food ingredients and supplies from **Approved Sources.**

An **approved source** is a supplier that is permitted by the Provincial Government, the local Health Authority, or the Federal Government.

If you're not sure if the supplier is permitted ask to see a copy of their food handling permit.

Receiving Food Products

Inspect all food products before accepting them into your facility. When inspecting food products check the following safety items:

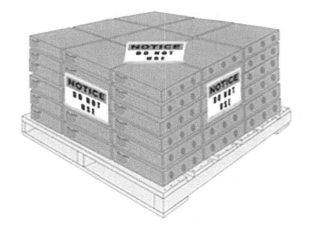

- The delivery vehicle should be clean and sanitary
- No packages are damaged
- There is no evidence of pest damage
- Food items are not past their expiration date
- Frozen food is frozen solid with no evidence of thawing. You can usually tell if food thawed and re-frozen if it is partially frozen and or there are excessive ice crystals on the food.
- Cold food products are at a temperature of 4°C/40°F or colder. An infrared thermometer can be very handy in this situation because it can give fast temperature reading.

Spoiled food products

Do not accept meat and meat products if they appear spoiled. Spoiled meat and meat products can have:

- Slime on the surface of the meat
- Discolouration
- Change in odor

Signs of spoilage in any food product especially in meat and products from animal origin can mean temperature abuse which can make the food not safe to eat.

Reject all food products that are damaged, expired, or appear to be temperature abused (thawed and re-frozen, appear to be spoiled or are not colder than 4°C/40°F when you receive it).

If food cannot be sent back with the delivery driver:

- Put the food in a separate storage area
- Hang a big clear sign stating
  "NOT FOR USE"
- Contact the supplier and arrange for pick-up of the food from your facility
- Speak to the supplier and ensure that problems do not persist.

If problems persist - find a different supplier.

Caution: Some food packaging such as shiny plastics can cause a false reading by the infrared thermometer.

Your notes:

Storage & FIFO

2 **Goal**

The goal of this section is to understand how cold or frozen food is protected from contamination in storage.

Things to Remember *Cook product is always on top*
raw product always on the bottom

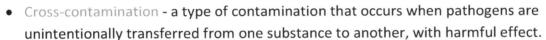

- Pathogens can contaminate and/or grow to harmful levels in storage if temperatures of perishable foods are not controlled and food is kept out of the Danger Zone.
- Perishable food items can be contaminated in cold storage if not protected and handled safely.
- Cross-contamination - a type of contamination that occurs when pathogens are unintentionally transferred from one substance to another, with harmful effect.
- Stock that is not used by its' "expiry date" could make customers ill.

First-In First-Out (FIFO)

- First In First Out or FIFO, is the method of shifting old stock to the front to be used **first** and new stock placed in the back to be used next.
- Read the "Expiry or Use by Dates" when storing food to make sure you are using the older products first.

Important Messages on Food Storage

In the fridge (cold storage):

- Store <u>raw meat</u>, <u>seafood</u>, <u>poultry</u>, or any <u>raw food from animal origin</u> below

ready-to-eat food, such as cooked dishes, vegetables, or fruits.
- Cover all food products in the cooler or freezer.
- Using sealed containers with label showing the date food was made or expiry date is recommended.
- Separate coolers could also be used to separate ready to eat food from raw uncooked food from animal origin.

In the freezer:

- Food is frozen at **0°C (32°C)**
- For quality reasons, freezer temperature is maintained at **-18°C (0°F)**
- Freezing will not kill bacteria and some viruses can also survive freezing
- Food stored in the freezer should also be covered and protected from contamination.
- Freezers must be maintained regularly
- It is also recommended that the de-frost cycle occur at night when it is not busy to avoid food temperature warming too quickly if the freezer door is being opened constantly.

Dry storage:

- Store all dry products off the floor and in pest proof "food-grade" containers. This will ensure proper cleaning takes place.
- Food grade containers are containers that are designed to safely hold food. Not all containers can be used to store food as some containers can leak dangerous chemicals into the food.
- To know if a container is food grade – check the manufacturer instructions.
- As a good rule, if a container was used for food, such as ice-cream buckets, it is food grade.

- Throw away products with damaged packaging. Damaged packaging such as damaged cans or broken flour bags may mean that the food is contaminated and is unsafe for use.
- Label all food that you remove from original packaging with the name and a "Use by Date" or its' "expiry date".
- Storage areas must be kept clean to prevent a pest infestation.

Caution: Damaged Cans can be especially dangerous! Damaged cans have the potential to allow the growth of a dangerous Pathogen called Clostridium Botulinum. This pathogen can cause Botulism Intoxication.

This type of intoxication is very dangerous and can often lead to serious neurological symptoms and even death!

Utensil Storage:

Reusable utensils such as knives, forks and spoons must be stored with the business end down.

This will make sure that they are handled properly and not contaminated after being washed and sanitized.

Hanging utensils can also work to make sure utensils are handled appropriately.

Non-reusable utensils such as plastic knives, forks and spoons should be kept in their original packaging until they are ready to be used.

Your notes:

Module 5

Food Handler Hygiene

The goal of this section is to help you understand how food handler hygiene is crucial to preventing food-borne illness.

Food Handler Hygiene

 1 **Goal**

The goal of this section is to help you understand how **food handler hygiene is crucial to preventing food-borne illness.**

Things to Remember

- Food handlers can transmit foodborne illness to their customers if they handle food while they are sick.

- Employees that have been ill should not return to work for at least 48 hours after their symptoms are gone or as advised by their doctor.

- People may still be carrying the disease-causing microorganism even after symptoms are gone. This person is called a "**carrier**".

Symptoms of foodborne illness:

- Diarrhea
- Vomiting
- Nausea
- Upset Stomach
- Fever
- Jaundice (yellowing of the skin)

Do your part for Safe Food:

- ☐ If you have any of the foodborne illness symptoms **DO NOT** report to work.
- ☐ Report any foodborne illness symptoms to your supervisor immediately.
- ☐ Encourage good personal hygiene for all food handlers

Be aware that some foodborne illnesses do not have obvious symptoms. This is why consistently following good personal hygiene policies and procedures are very important!

Safe personal hygiene practices

- Wear clean clothes.
- Appropriate hair control using a hair net, hats, or other ways of making sure the hair is controlled. Hair control is important to prevent the individual from having to touch or adjust their hair during food handling. This prevents cross-contamination of food and food-contact surfaces.
- No Jewellery (plain wedding bands that don't have any stones maybe allowed)
- Food handlers are careful not to touch their face, hair, or any other parts of their body when handling food.
- Food handlers should not smoke, eat, or chew gum when preparing food. All of these actions may lead to cross-contamination.
- Practice proper hand washing.

Supervisors and Managers 48 hours after

- ☐ Supervisors and managers have to watch, coach, and ensure that the staff are following safe personal hygiene practices
- ☐ Employees need to feel comfortable talking to their managers and supervisors: to do this, managers should make sure that employees are aware of the signs of Foodborne Illness and that they report them as soon as possible
- ☐ Having paid sick leave or at the very least not punishing staff for calling in sick is a good start
- ☐ If an employee informs a manager or a supervisor that they have any of the symptoms described above, the manager should send the employee home and for medical testing and/or treatment

Handling Food Safety Complaints

Food safety related complaints from the public should not be ignored. Although some complaints may not be legitimate, it is important for a food business to take all food safety related complaints seriously.

Here are some recommended steps to handling a foodborne illness complaint:

Step #1

Thank the customer for coming forward with the complaint. Do not offer an opinion on the incident but proceed to ask questions and get more details.

Step #2

Collect as much information about the incident as possible. Here are some questions that can be asked:

- Name and phone number or other contact information such as email of the complainant
- Details of the incident. Get as many details as possible
- Ask if there were other people affected
- Ask if they received medical attention and if any laboratory testing occurred

Step #3

Inform the complainant that you will investigate the complaint (or send complaint to management) and will get back to them.

Encourage them to seek medical attention if they haven't already

Step #4

If the complaint involves foodborne illness symptoms such as vomiting and diarrhea and especially if it involves a number of individuals, then contact the local health inspector and inform them of the details of the complaint.

Notes:

The health inspector can be a great resource in these situations as they can help identify if the complaint is likely or not.

Every food business should track and document customer complaints. This is helpful because it allows managers to review complaints and identify any trends or repetitive issues.

Handy Hygiene

Things to Remember

Hand washing is one of the most important ways of preventing harmful microbes from getting onto food and contact surfaces.

It is also one of the most important ways to prevent the spread of foodborne illnesses and other diseases that can be passed from one person to the other.

How to Ensure Proper Hand Washing?

☐ Have a designated Hand-wash sink and ensure there is hot/cold water, soap and paper towels. Nail brushes are also recommended.

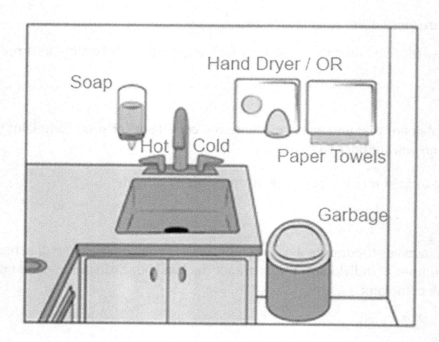

Follow proper handwashing steps:

Step #1: Wet your hands with warm water and apply a generous amount of soap to your hands.

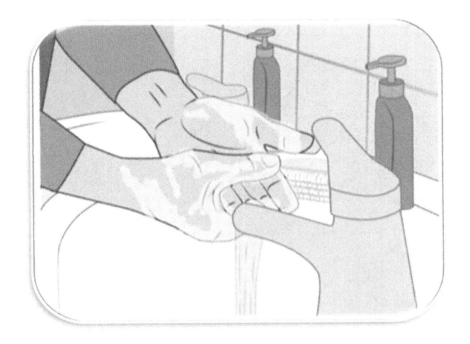

Step #2: Clean under your fingernails and use a brush.

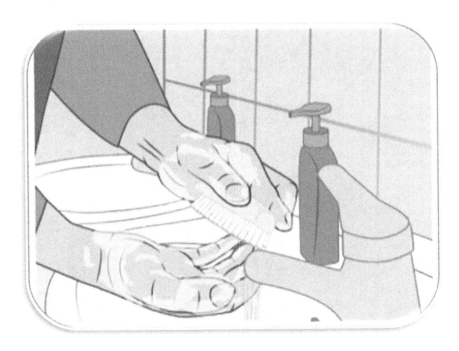

Step #3: Rub hands together for at least twenty seconds – don't forget between your fingers and back of your hand. Tip: Try singing "happy birthday" to ensure you are rubbing your hands long enough.

Rinse hands thoroughly under running water.

Step #4: Dry hands using paper towels and discard into garbage bin.

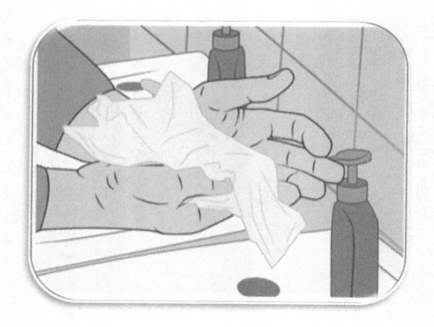

When to wash your hands:

- ☐ After using the washroom
- ☐ After a break or after eating and drinking
- ☐ After handling raw foods such as meat, poultry, seafood and raw vegetables
- ☐ Between switching tasks
- ☐ After sneezing or coughing
- ☐ After smoking or chewing tobacco
- ☐ After taking out the garbage
- ☐ After cleaning tables or any other type of cleaning
- ☐ After touching your face

Wearing Jewelry:

Jewellery can harbour (hide) dirt and bacteria and cannot be cleaned properly.

- ☐ Remove rings, watches, ear rings, nose rings and all other jewellery when handling food.
- ☐ Wedding rings that cannot be easily removed maybe allowed, but special care should be taken to clean around and under the ring. Gloves may also be used in along with proper hand washing.

Your Notes:

Glove Use

Things to Remember

For Bare Hands

☐ Nails must be kept short and clean.

☐ Artificial nail and other nail decorations should not be worn during food preparation and general food handling.

☐ Any cuts, sores, or wounds must be covered with a bandage and a glove must be worn over the bandage

For Gloved Hands

• Wash hands prior to gloving

• Change gloves between each task (e.g. handling food and handling cash)

• Change gloves between handling raw foods, such as raw meat and handling of ready-to-eat foods, such as cooked food.

Hand Hygiene Notes:

1. Ensure new staff are aware of and follow the hand hygiene policy

2. Provide a hand wash station at a more convenient location

3. Ensure staff are aware of the glove use policy.

4. Ensure you have a written glove use policy.

5. Have comfortable gloves readily available.

6. Some individuals maybe allergic to latex gloves. It is important to ensure that alternative glove types are also available.

Hint: Posting signs in food handling areas about proper hand washing and glove use is recommended as a reminder for all food handlers.

Customer Service

Things to Remember

- Use serving utensils so as to keep hands away from the food.
- Only use clean and sanitized utensils.
- Handle flatware and utensils by the handles.

- Glassware and dishes have to be held so hands do not touch the area where the food or the customer's mouth will touch.

Never put fingers inside glassware before service since it will contaminate the glass by the germs in your hand.

- Do NOT use cracked, chipped or broken plates or cutlery.
  - Broken plates and other cutlery pose a physical hazard and can harm your customers.

Broken or chipped plates pose a physical hazard.

Module 6

Safe Food Handling

The goal of this section is to outline Safe Food Handling and learn how to accurately measure temperatures using clean and calibrated probe thermometers.

Temperature Monitoring and Calibrating a Thermometer

 1 Goal

The goal of this section is to outline Safe Food Handling and learn how to accurately measure temperatures using clean and calibrated probe thermometers.

Things to Remember

Temperature control is one of the most important topics in this section. Before learning the different ways to handle food, it is vital for all food handlers to understand how to take food temperatures properly and safely.

Taking food temperatures with a thermometer is the best way to know if food is at the right temperature. However, thermometers can transfer microbes into food if not properly cleaned and sanitized before use.

An improperly calibrated thermometer will not provide accurate temperature readings and poses a risk to food safety by misleading food handlers.

Using the Thermometer

A probe thermometer should be properly cleaned and sanitized before inserting it into food. This step is also important when using the thermometer between different food types.

Clean the thermometer using:

- Alcohol based wipes

OR

- Wash with soap and water and sanitize using an approved sanitizer (follow directions on dishwashing section on proper dishwashing and sanitizing)

Calibrating the Thermometer

- Every thermometer should be calibrated or checked regularly.
- Two ways of Calibrating a thermometer:
  - Boiling water method

    OR

  - Ice water method

Boiling Water Method

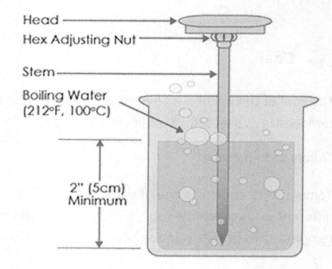

1. Bring a clean container of water to a rolling boil.
2. Place thermometer probe into boiling water for at least one minute. Do not touch the bottom of the container with the thermometer.
3. The thermometer should read 212° F or 100oC (+/- 2°F).

Ice Water Method
Same as Boiling Water except using ice water

1. Add crushed ice and water to a clean container to form a watery slush.
2. Place thermometer probe into slush for at least one minute.
3. The thermometer should read about 32°F 0°C (+/- 2°F) or 0°C.

Thermometers found to be inaccurate (i.e. do not measure within +/- 2°F of the actual temperature) should either be manually adjusted or serviced by a professional.

Discard and replace thermometers that are constantly out of range – i.e. do not measure within +/-2°F.

Your notes:

Cross-Contamination

 Goal

The goal of this section is to understand how to control cross-contamination of food items.

Things to Remember

Cross Contamination is the transfer of contaminants from a surface or a person to the food. Food can be contaminated from microbes, physical contamination such as metal objects, and chemical contamination.

Unclean equipment, people, and utensils can contaminate food and cause illness or injury.

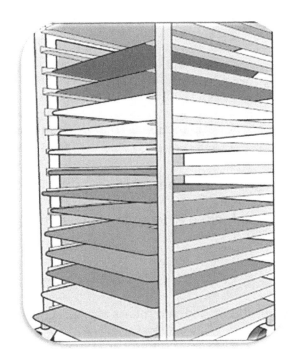

Controlling Cross-Contamination

- Use a separate area in the kitchen and designated cutting boards for raw meat, poultry, seafood or raw foods from animal origin.
- **NEVER** use the same cutting board for preparing cooked or ready to eat food after it's been used to prepare raw foods without first properly cleaning and sanitizing it.
- Only use food-grade containers or bags for food storage. Black garbage bags are not approved food-grade material.
- All chemical bottles and maintenance lubricants should be labeled and stored in a secure area away from food preparation.
- Discard food packaging as soon as possible to avoid cross contamination of physical objects such as staples or packaging straps.
- Discard broken utensils, equipment (e.g. strainers), and containers. Broken equipment is a physical hazard to food.

Your notes:

Cooking

 3 Goal

The goal of this section is to understand how potentially hazardous foods are cooked properly and to appropriate temperatures.

Things to Remember

Cooking food to appropriate temperatures ensures that harmful bacteria do not cause food-borne illness.

Ground/Processed Meats

Ground or processed meats are **<u>NEVER</u>** served rare or medium rare.

- The internal temperature must always reach **74°C (165°F).**
- All processed meats such as rolled joints, tenderized meat, and others must always be cooked to internal temperature of **74°C (165°F).**
- This is because in these types of food products microbe contamination can be inside and throughout the meat.

Use a probe thermometer to check the internal temperature of food!

Whole Cuts and Whole Joints of Meat

Whole cuts of muscle meat such as steaks can be served to preference (e.g. rare or medium rare) as long as the outside of the meat is seared.

This is because microbial contamination on the outside of the meat is destroyed by searing and is not mixed inside the meat like ground or processed products.

Poultry

Poultry is **NEVER** served rare or medium rare.

- Pieces of poultry such as chicken breast must reach an internal temperature of **74°C (165°F).**
- Whole pieces of poultry require a higher internal temperature **85°C (185°F).**

This is because a whole piece of poultry has higher fat content and higher heat is needed to destroy harmful microbes.

Food Item	Required Internal Temperature
Poultry (Pieces)	74°C (165°F)
Poultry (whole)	85°C (185°F)

Fish and Shellfish

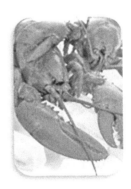

- Fin Fish is cooked to **70°C (158°F).** Look for the color of the fish to turn opaque and flaky.
- Shellfish is cooked to **74°C (165°F)** When cooking shellfish, such as shrimp, crab or lobster, look for pearly or opaque color change.
- Prawns will turn from blue-grey to pink
- Scallops become milky white and firm when cooked properly.
- Before cooking mussels or clams throw away any open or damaged shells, as they are not safe to eat.
- To check that a mussel or clam is **cooked properly**, ensure that the shell is **open**. If the shell is not open, cook longer or discard it.

Liquid Dishes

- Liquid dishes such as soups and gravies are cooked when they come to a rolling boil.
- Stir the liquid to ensure that no cold spots are present.

NOTE: Some information is adapted from befoodsafe.ca! For more information visit - www.befoodsafe.ca/en-temperature.asp

Sushi and Food Safety

- Raw fish can contain parasites that can infect humans if not adequately controlled.
- Freezing if done correctly, can destroy parasites found in fish.
- This freezing to destroy parasites is often done at the manufacturer / supplier of the fish

If parasites are controlled at the supplier:
- o Obtain written verification that the fish has been frozen to appropriate temperature to control parasites
- o Safely handle the fish using safe food handling practices

If parasites are controlled at the food facility / food service level:
- o Fish must be frozen at a temperature of -20°C (-4°F) or colder for 7 days OR
- o Fish must be stored at a temperature of -35°C (-31°F) for 15 hours

Your notes:

Cooling

 Goal

The goal of this section is to understand how hot food is cooled safely.

Things to Remember

Once food is cooked, harmful bacteria can re-grow if the food is kept in the temperature Danger Zone!

The Danger Zone is temperatures between 4°C to 60°C – this is where pathogens grow rapidly.

Important Messages for Cooling

- The goal here is to cool hot foods as quickly as possible and place in the refrigerator.
- Hot foods have to be cooled:
    - from **60°C (140°F)** to **20°C (68°F)** within 2 hours or less.
      AND
    - from **20°C (68°F)** to **4°C (40°F)** within 4 hours or less.

Cooling foods can be done by:

- Stirring food often as it is being cooled
- Put hot food in shallow containers (preferably metal containers because metal cools faster) and stir often
- Use an Ice-Bath method. This involves putting a metal container inside a bigger container filled with ice. The ice on the outside will cool the food inside the metal container by absorbing the heat.
- Place hot food in a blast freezer until cool and then transfer to refrigerator
- Place hot food on a rack to improve air circulation which will help cool foods faster.

Your notes:

Hot Holding

5 **Goal**

The goal of this section is to understand how to safely store hot food limiting pathogen bacterial growth.

Things to Remember

Food in the Danger zone will allow microbes to grow quickly and cause illness.

The Danger Zone is temperatures between **4°C to 60°C** – this is where pathogens grow rapidly.

Important Messages for Cooling

- Always reheat food before putting it in hot holding unit! <u>NEVER</u> use the hot holding unit to reheat food.

- Turn on hot holding equipment and let it heat up <u>BEFORE</u> placing the reheated food inside it.

- Once food is placed in the hot holding unit, check the temperature often to ensure it is maintained at **60°C (140°F)** or hotter.

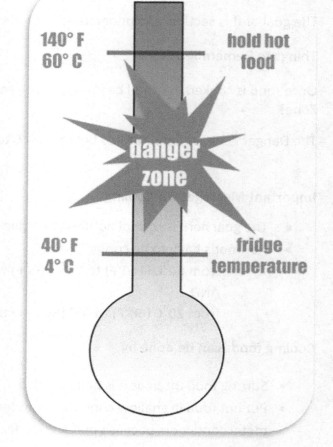

- Do not pile food too high on hot holding unit because the top part of the food will not reach 60°C (140°F).

- Stir food often to ensure that the heat is distributed and there is no "cold spots".

- Food kept in hot holding units should not be used again but either consumed immediately or discarded.

Use a probe thermometer to check the internal temperature of food!

Your notes:

Re-Heating

6 Goal

The goal of this section is to understand how to re-heat food to appropriate temperatures.

Things to Remember

If food is not reheated properly, harmful microbes might survive and cause illness.

Important Messages for Cooling

Make sure to use proper reheating equipment when reheating food. Equipment such as:

- Ovens
- Pots and pans on stove
- Microwaves
- Barbeque
- Food should be reheated to internal temperature of 74°C/165°F.
- Stir or mix food through out to ensure that heat reaches every part of the food and that there are no cold spots. This is especially important when using microwaves as they may not heat the food evenly
- Serve reheated food immediately or keep hot at 60°C/ 140°F.

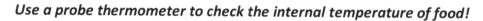

Use a probe thermometer to check the internal temperature of food!

A note about Microwaves

- Only use plastic containers designed for microwave use.
- Glass containers are sometimes better suited for reheating food in the microwave.
- Stir or mix food through out to ensure that heat reaches every part of the food and that there are no cold spots.

Thawing Food

 Goal

The goal of this section is to understand how to safely thaw food.

Things to Remember

- Food thawed improperly can cause cross-contamination of raw juices on ready to eat food.

- Improperly thawed food or partially frozen food cooks unevenly and may allow harmful microbial growth to cause illness.

Important Messages for Thawing

- Plan ahead and place frozen food items in the cooler over night to thaw.

- Defrost food in a way to prevent dripping or cross contamination in storage. For example, place frozen food in a closed container on a tray or a dish and store **BELOW** ready to eat foods.

- Thawing food at room temperature is **not** approved.

Proper thawing methods:

- Thaw frozen food in the refrigerator overnight

- Use the microwave to thaw food only if the food will be cooked immediately.

- Place packaged frozen foods under cold running water.

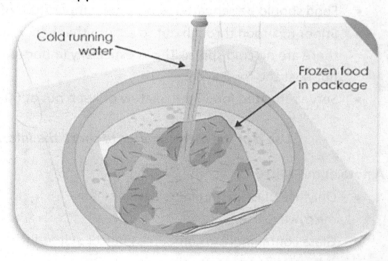

Check that food is thawed before cooking:

- Check to make sure the centre of the food is defrosted

- Check to ensure that poultry joints move easily indicating it's been thawed throughout

Off-site Catering

8 Goal

The goal of this section is to understand how to ensure food is safely handled when catering food offsite.

Things to Remember

- Food can become contaminated in many ways during transportation. Chemical, physical, and biological contamination is possible if food is not handled safely.

- Temperature abuse or food kept in the Danger Zone (4^0C to 60^0C) can result in harmful microbial growth causing illness.

Important Messages for Off-site Catering

Protect all food during transport:

- Keep the vehicle where food is transported clean and free from dust, and other contaminants such as chemicals and tools.

- Always keep ready to eat food separate from raw food.

- Do not allow animals in the vehicle used to transport food.

Maintain temperature control in the following ways:

- Use insulated containers to keep hot food above 60^0C/140^0F.

- Portable coolers can be used to transport food cold. Adding ice to the coolers can keep the temperature below 4^0C/40^0F.

Plan ahead

- Plan to transport and serve food in as little time as possible. This will ensure that food temperature is kept either cold (4^0C/40^0F or colder) or hot (60^0C/140^0F) and **NOT** in the Danger Zone.

- Take extra utensils on-site if there is no availability to wash and sanitize utensils properly.

- Know what facilities are available at the catering site. For example, is there reheating equipment, refrigeration, hand washing equipment, cleaning equipment etc....?

Food Allergens

 Goal

The goal of this section is to help you understand what the most common food allergies are, and how to be allergen safe.

Things to Remember

A food allergy occurs when an individual's own immune system attacks the body because of a food ingredient the person was exposed to.

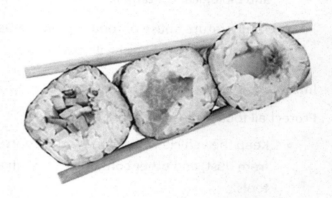

It is very important that customers have accurate information on whether a food contains specific allergens, or if you handle this allergen in your facility. Allergic reactions will defer between one individual and the other.

Common Food Allergens

Health Canada and the Canadian Food Inspection Agency have listed the most common food allergens, called *priority* allergens:

1. Peanuts

2. Soy

3. Eggs

4. Sesame Seeds

5. Milk

6. Seafood (fish, crustaceans and shellfish)

7. Tree Nuts

8. Sulphites

9. Wheat

10. Mustard

Allergic Reactions

Some allergic individuals can have a life threatening reaction to an allergen that may result in death if not treated immediately.

- "Anaphylactic Shock" ---**Occurs within minutes of eating the food**.
- Other allergic reactions can be less severe and will depend on the individual.
- Food Allergies affect as many as 5 or 6 % of young children and 3-4% of adults in westernized countries.

*NOTE: Allergic reaction is **NOT** the same as food sensitivity. Food sensitivities are typically less severe and cause discomforts and other symptoms that vary from one person to the other.*

Your notes:

How to Control Allergens and Deal with Allergic Customers

1. **TALK TO YOUR CUSTOMERS**---If your customers tell you they have allergies to a certain food ingredient, talk to them about what menu items may be appropriate for them.

2. **NEVER GUESS** ---If you are not sure if a menu item has a certain allergen in it or not, do not guess. Tell the customer that you don't know and they will appreciate it.

3. **DEVELOP A LIST OF INGREDIENTS**---You should have a list of ingredients for all your menu items. Remember to keep track of ingredients in your menu that are processed outside your facility.

4. **USE PRECAUTIONS TO PREVENT CROSS-CONTACT**---Before preparing the meal for an allergic individual, the chef must begin by washing hands thoroughly. If gloves are used, then a fresh pair of gloves is put on after hand washing.

   a. All equipment and utensils used in meal preparation must be cleaned and sanitized before beginning the meal preparations.

   b. Only fresh ingredients should be used for garnish.

   c. A source of cross-contact can be cooking oils. For example, the same oil is used to deep fry shrimp that is used to deep fry vegetarian spring rolls. When the cook uses the same oil to fry the shrimp that is then used for frying the spring rolls, someone with an allergy to shrimp may have an allergic reaction to the spring rolls because of proteins released in the oil.

   d. NOTE: Food safety experts recommend that someone (ideally the manager) who is familiar with allergen procedures be the point of contact for all allergen related inquiries.

Case Study

A guest in an ethnic restaurant informed the waiter that he had a peanut allergy and asked if their spring rolls contained peanuts. The waiter did not check with the manager but told the guest he was sure that there were no peanut products in the spring rolls. He also was sure the cook had not fried the spring rolls in peanut oil. The waiter informed the guest that the spring rolls were peanut-free.

There were no other discussions with the guest on the possibility of cross-contact with peanuts in the facility. The waiter did not ask how serious his allergy was to peanuts. The guest took a few bites of the egg roll and quickly developed an anaphylactic allergic reaction. The reaction was so severe that the guest died.

Someone later discovered that the chef had decided to use peanut butter as glue, to glue the ends of the spring rolls.

How could this have been prevented?

This incident could have been prevented this tragedy---and saved a life---if the waiter had first asked the manager if there were peanuts in the spring rolls. The manager should have known that there was peanut butter on the spring rolls and informed the guest of this fact.

Your notes:

Case Study

Unsafe hot-holding procedure

A chef at a small motel was known for her delicious lunch Buffett. Especially popular was the Currie hot dishes. She would make most of the dishes the night before, refrigerate them and then serve them the next morning in her buffet.

One of the kitchen staff members would go around and check the temperature of the food in the hot holding dishes towards the end of the lunch period when things have slowed a little bit.

Is this an appropriate way to ensure food is safe?

Your notes:

Mobile and Temporary Food Service

10 **Goal**

The goal of this section is to help you understand the most common food safety challenges of mobile and temporary food service operations and how to control them.

Things to Remember

- Mobile and temporary food operations require a Food Permit or approval of special event from the local Health Authority
- All food safety controls for a restaurant also apply to mobile and temporary food businesses.

Food Safety Challenges of Mobile Food Businesses

- Owners have to ensure infrastructure of the mobile is regularly completed. For example, filling water tanks, emptying waste water, finding and planning for power sources.
- Limited space is often a large challenge for storing, cooking, and handling food.
- Limited equipment such as smaller sinks, fridges, etc. require more planning ahead of service time to ensure safe food handling
- Fewer staff means the same person could be doing multiple duties which may lead to cross contamination

Safe Operation of Mobile Food Businesses

- Plan ahead and make sure the infrastructure like water and power will be available during service
- Educate all food handlers on safe food handling practices
- Remove anything that is not part of the food service to make space and reduce clutter
- Regularly inspect the mobile or temporary operation to ensure that the infrastructure like water, waster water and power are available and that food handlers are following proper food handling and safe hygiene practices
- Thoroughly clean mobile or temporary equipment between events/service times.

Module 7

Cleaning, Sanitizing, Dishwashing

The goal of this section is to understand the approved methods for cleaning and sanitizing required in a food business.

Cleaning and Sanitizing

1 **Goal**

The goal of this section is to understand the approved methods for cleaning and sanitizing required in a food business.

Things to Remember

Dirty surfaces and equipment may allow microbes to grow and contaminate food. Dirty conditions can also allow pests like mice, and cockroaches to multiply and spread disease.

Proper Cleaning Procedures

1. Pre-Clean
2. Wash
3. Rinse
4. Sanitize
5. Air Dry

Proper Cleaning Procedures:

Step #1: Pre-Clean – Remove all visible dirt and food from equipment, utensil, food contact surfaces and non-food contact surfaces.

Step #2: Wash – Use detergent to wash the surface. This is an important step because it cleans the surface from dirt, grease, or food that may have become stuck.

Step #3: Rinse – Rinse with clean water to remove soap and other debris from surface.

Step #4: Sanitize – Sanitize with an approved sanitizer

Step #5: Air Dry – Allow the surface air dry.

Store utensils properly, with the handle extended above the container, or on a clean, sanitized food-contact surface.

What is cleaning and sanitizing?

- The term cleaning or clean means to remove all food residues, dirt and other materials.
  - Cleaning is often done using a soap and water solution.
  - Cleaning is different than sanitizing
- Sanitizing is the killing of harmful microorganisms.
  - Sanitizing brings the level of microorganisms down so that they do not cause disease in humans.
  - Sanitizing is done using a sanitizer and cleaning solution
  - In order for sanitizing to be effective, the surface has to be cleaned first so that all food residues or other foreign materials are removed.

What is a Sanitizer?

A sanitizer is a chemical used for killing harmful microorganisms on a surface. While sanitizing does not kill ALL microorganisms, it reduces their numbers to safe levels.

There are four main categories of approved sanitizers:

1. Heat sanitizing

2. Chlorine sanitizing

3. Quaternary Ammonium Compounds – also known as Quats

4. Iodine

Sanitizers Explained:

<u>Heat Sanitizing</u> is accomplished once the temperature of the surface reaches <u>74°C (165°F).</u> At this temperature, harmful microorganisms are reduced to acceptable levels. This temperature is usually only available in high temperature dishwashers.

<u>Chlorine Sanitizing</u> is accomplished once the concentration reaches <u>100ppm.</u> At this ~~200~~ concentration, harmful microorganisms are reduced to acceptable levels.

<u>Quaternary Ammonium Compounds (or Quats) Sanitizing</u> is accomplished once the concentration reaches <u>200 ppm.</u> – ~~400~~

<u>Iodine Sanitizing</u> is accomplished once the concentration is between <u>12.5 – 25ppm.</u>

Sanitizer Summary Table:

Sanitizing Type	Required concentration/temperature/contact time	How do you test it?
Heat	77°C (171°F) for at least 2 minutes	*Thermometers can be used to ensure this temperature is reached.* *It is important to ensure that the thermometers being used are calibrated regularly*
Chlorine	*100ppm (immersion) for at least 2 minutes* *AND* *200ppm for clean in place (clean in place is surfaces that do not get immersed into a sink nor go through a commercial dishwasher.*	*Test strips provided by the chemical suppliers.*
Quaternary Ammonium (Quats)	*200ppm (immersion) for at least 2 minutes* *AND* *400ppm for clean in place (clean in place is surfaces that do not get immersed into a sink nor go through a commercial dishwasher.*	*Test strips provided by the chemical suppliers.*
Iodine	*A range of 12.5 to 25 ppm*	*Test strips provided by the chemical suppliers.*

Note: Iodine use has been on decline because of its tendency to stain food equipment.

Handling Cleaning Chemicals

Cleaning chemicals can contaminate food if not stored and handled them properly.

Chemicals not used correctly will not be effective in destroying pathogens.

Misuse of chemicals can also result in injury or negative health effects.

Creating a cleaning chemical list will help you control chemical use, keep food safe and protect you and other staff members.

CLEANING CHEMICAL LIST: EXAMPLE TEMPLATE

Chemical Name	Use in Facility	Concentration	Mixing instructions	Concentration Monitoring	How Applied
YZ Sanitizer	Sanitizer to be used for all equipment that is not washed in dishwasher	200ppm	Automated from pump	Use test strips and measure concentration	Pump directly into bucket and use.

Important Things to Remember:

- ☐ Read and follow all manufacturers' instructions on how to mix chemicals.

- ☐ Store chemicals away from food. Chemicals should be stored in a cabinet on a lower shelf away from food and food packaging materials.

- ☐ Train everyone to label clearly all chemical spray bottles or containers. Labelling chemical bottles will ensure that people will use them correctly.

- ☐ Using a separate cleaning area with a drain is recommended to prevent chemical contamination.

Designing a Cleaning Schedule

Different parts of the kitchen should be cleaned differently and on different frequencies. A cleaning schedule can organize the cleaning and help in training of staff on proper cleaning methods.

- ☐ Walk through your establishment and write down everything that you would need to clean.

- ☐ Determine how often you want each item cleaned i.e. the frequency of cleaning

- ☐ Write out how workers will conduct this cleaning ---detailed instruction that systematically outline how each item is cleaned. Remember to include the types of chemicals to be used and chemical mixing/diluting instructions.

- ☐ Highlight items that are high-risk and ensure everyone is aware of the difference between high and low risk items.

High Risk Areas

High-risk items are those items that come in direct contact with food or food equipment. Here are some examples:

- ☐ Cleaning cloths
- ☐ Food mixers, slicers, and grinders
- ☐ All hand contact surfaces such as door handles
- ☐ Food surfaces such as work tables or large in-place cutting boards

Low Risk Areas

Low risk areas are those that do not come in contact with food.

Other low risk items reach a high enough temperature to kill harmful bacteria, such as ovens. Examples of low risk items:

- ☐ Ceilings
- ☐ Display cabinets
- ☐ Dry storage areas
- ☐ Floors
- ☐ Walls
- ☐ Staff areas
- ☐ Ventilation
- ☐ Garbage disposal areas

Cleaning Cloths

Cleaning cloths, if not handled properly, can be a source of cross-contamination.

Handling Cleaning Cloths:

- ☐ During the shift, keep cleaning cloths in sanitizing solution when they are not in use. This will ensure pathogens do not survive and cross-contaminate other surfaces.

- ☐ Overnight, cleaning cloths must be laundered and stored dry.

- ☐ Ensure there is enough supply of clean cleaning cloths available

- ☐ Replace worn out cleaning cloths

Liquid Waste

- Janitorial room where cleaning equipment is stored should be located away from food and food storage areas.
- Brooms, mops, pails and cleaning chemicals are typically stored in the Janitorial room.
- The janitorial room should also be equipped with a drain to allow the save disposal of mop water and other liquid waste such as dirty sanitizer bucket water.

Liquid waste from mop water or cleaning buckets contains pathogens and filth that can cross contaminate food and cause a foodborne illness.

Your notes:

Dishwashing – Manual & Mechanical

2 Goal

The goal of this section is to understand proper dishwashing procedures and ensure that equipment and utensils are safe for use in a food facility.

Things to Remember

Following proper dishwashing procedures reduces harmful microorganisms to acceptable levels.

Proper dishwashing can be done manually or using a mechanical dishwasher.

Manual Dishwashing

With manual dishwashing, a three-compartment sink method is utilized.

A two-compartment sink can also be used in some cases. Whether the health department allows the two-compartment sink depends on the types of utensils utilized in the kitchen.

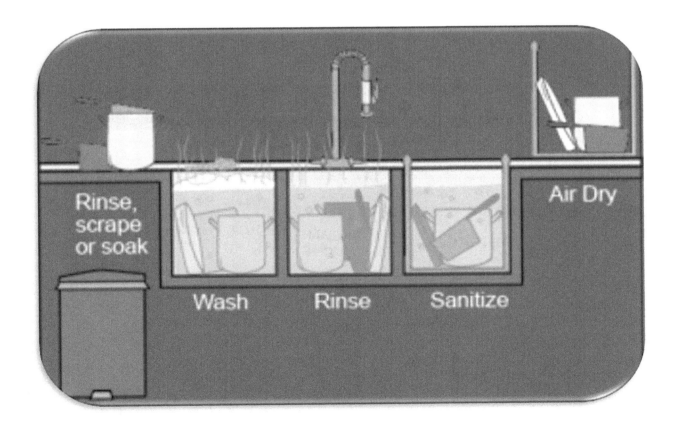

Steps for Manual Dishwashing:

Step #1: Rinse, Scrape or Soak: removing food debris prepares the dishes for proper cleaning and sanitizing. Food and other organic debris reduces the effectiveness of sanitizers.

Step #2: Wash: the first compartment sink is filled with soap and water. Soap/detergent helps to fully remove tiny organic materials and prepares the dishes for sanitizing. Wash water temperature must be **45.0°C**

Step #3: Rinse: the second compartment sink is filled with **clean water**. This removes the soap and organic material and gets dishes ready for sanitizing.

For sinks with only two compartments, this step can be completed by running water to rinse the dishes off in the first sink. Rinse water temperature must be **45.0°C**

Step#4: Sanitize: this sink is filled with a sanitizer water solution. This is designed to sanitize dishes and reduce pathogens to acceptable levels. Refer to **Sanitizer Table Summary** for appropriate concentrations.

Sanitizing requirements:

1. HOT WATER: **Over 77°C for 2 minutes**
2. **Chlorine Solution: 100ppm**
3. **Quaternary Ammonium Solution: 200ppm**

Step#5: Air Dry: letting dishes air dry is the last step and ensures dishes are ready to be used.

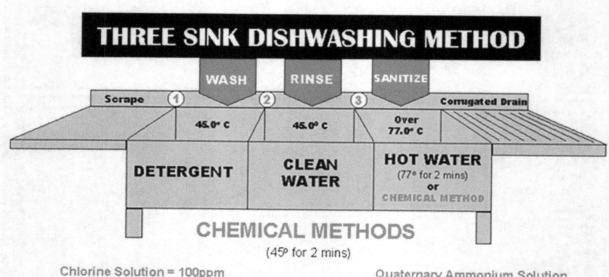

THREE SINK DISHWASHING METHOD

Scrape — ① WASH 45.0° C — ② RINSE 45.0° C — ③ SANITIZE Over 77.0° C — Corrugated Drain

DETERGENT | CLEAN WATER | HOT WATER (77° for 2 mins) or CHEMICAL METHOD

CHEMICAL METHODS
(45° for 2 mins)

Chlorine Solution = 100ppm
Dilution of 5% Bleach (Chlorine) approximately
• one tbsp. per gallon of water
• 1/2 ounce per gallon of water
• 1/2 tsp. per litre of water
• 2ml per litre of water

Quaternary Ammonium Solution
(Quats) = 200ppm
Dilution of Quats
Follow manufactures instructions

Mechanical Dishwashing

Commercial dishwashers come in many different shapes and sizes.

Some have chemical disinfectants and others utilize a hot water booster to achieve extremely high temperatures.

It is important to ensure that dishes are scraped well before putting them in the dishwasher.

This scraping will ensure proper cleaning and sanitizing as well as preventing food residue from becoming "baked" on the plates by the dishwasher temperature.

Troubleshooting Mechanical Dishwashers:

- ☐ Ensure that the dishwasher is on a regular maintenance program and is cleaned and monitored regularly
- ☐ It may be beneficial to have a regular contract with a service provider to maintain your machine and supply you with appropriate chemicals.
- ☐ High temperature dishwashers can sometimes take a few cycles to get the sanitizing temperature up to appropriate levels
- ☐ Use a test strip to check sanitizer concentrations.
- ☐ Double check sanitizing temperature and/or sanitizing concentrations <u>regularly</u>

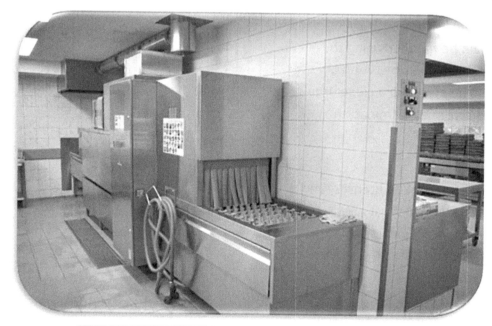

Picture source: Alberta Food Retail and Foodservices Code, 2003. Alberta Health

Mechanical Dishwashing Sanitizing Temperature/Concentrations:

High Temperature Sanitizing:

Wash temperature – 60°C (140°F) during the wash cycle. Most dishwashers will have gauges to display temperatures during the different cleaning and sanitizing cycles.

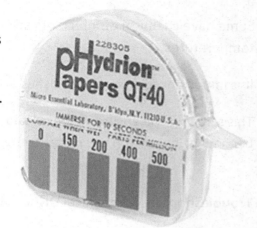

Sanitizing temperature - 82°C (180°F) during the rinse cycle. Again, check the proper gauge to ensure the temperature get high enough.

Chemical Sanitizing:

Approved Chemical sanitizers are:

- ☐ 100 ppm Chlorine Solution
- ☐ 200 ppm QUATS or Quaternary Ammonium Solution
- ☐ 12.5 to 25 ppm Iodine

Note: Each dishwasher is unique, always check the manufacturer's requirements to ensure it is being operated safely and properly. Your dishwasher will thank you!

Handline and Storage of Clean Utensils and Dishes:

- • Dishware should be air dried
- • Utensils should be handled using the handle and not the "business end".
- • Dishes should be stored in a clean area and protected from contamination

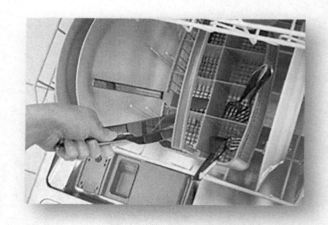

Note: Cracked, chipped or broken utensils, and equipment should be used and must be discarded. Broken or chipped plates and other dishwasher poses a physical hazard.

Single Service Utensils and Dishes:

- Single service utensils should be stored in their original packaging until used
- They are not designed to be re-used and therefore they should be discarded after use
-

Your notes:

Case Study

Monika is a manager at the Two Spoon restaurant, serving 200 people every day in two shifts. The restaurant prides itself on having a variety of healthy food options for their customers.

Monika is responsible for 5-kitchen staff and all the staff members do the cleaning. Kitchen cleaning and sanitation is important to Monika. She checks on the cleaning at the end of every day for daily cleaning, and on Sunday for the weekly cleaning.

Monika often gets frustrated when she notices that staff members failed to clean certain items. Here are the items that staff have trouble cleaning regularly or not at all:

- Meat Slicer not cleaned properly
- Refrigeration door handle
- Dry goods storage areas
- Ceilings in the kitchen
- Garbage bins inside the restaurant

What can Monika can do to make sure that staff members clean these items properly?

Things Monika can do:

- *Ensure that she list these items in her cleaning schedule and make sure they have appropriate cleaning frequency.*
- *Monika should then make sure that she trains her staff on how to conduct this cleaning properly. She can even post this schedule in the kitchen so staff can refer to if they forget how to clean a certain item.*
- *Finally, Monika needs to ensure that she is able to remember to check and make sure that staff members are cleaning these items on a regular basis. The staff can conduct this cleaning in many ways, but one way is for Monika to create a checklist and make sure that her employees use this checklist on a regular basis.*

Here is an example cleaning schedule.

Item	Frequency of Cleaning	Method of cleaning
Meat Slicer	After every use	☐ Disassemble machine and place smaller parts in the dishwasher. ☐ Remove obvious food residue with cleaning cloth. ☐ Wash the big parts with warm soapy water using Sunlight detergent (1capful per liter of water) ☐ Spray on Chlorine sanitizer (blue bottle) and leave for 1 min. ☐ Wipe clean with wet cloth ☐ Leave to air dry before next shift.
Refrigeration Door Handles	Daily	☐ Wash with warm soapy water using Sunlight detergent (1capful per liter of water) ☐ Rinse off with clean tap water ☐ Spray on sanitizer (blue bottle) and leave for 1 min. ☐ Wipe clean with wet cloth ☐ Leave to air dry before next shift.
Dry Goods Storage Areas	Every Sunday Afternoon	☐ Sweep floors using broom ☐ Remove cans and other containers off the shelves and wipe shelves using a wet cloth ☐ Check for any evidence of pests and report them to the manager. ☐ Check all goods for expired product and discard them. ☐ Mop the floor with soapy water and let air dry.
Garbage bins	Monthly	☐ Take bin to the mop sink and spray with soapy water. ☐ Rinse with clean water
Ceilings in the Kitchen	Every Three Months	☐ Standing on the ladder wipe down the ceiling over all food preparation areas. Note: Kitchen must not be in use. Only do this after restaurant is closed and all food is put away. ☐ Use a bucket of soapy water and a cleaning cloth to wipe down the ceiling over all food preparation areas.

Here is an example of a daily checklist. Monika can use a similar checklist for weekly cleaning, monthly and other frequencies as she decides.

Cleaning check list

Item	Monday	Tuesday	Wednesday	Thursday	Friday	Saturday	Sunday
Daily Cleaning							
Meat Slicer							
Floors moped							
Etc....							
Weekly Cleaning							
Dry Good Storage							
Etc....							
Monthly Cleaning							
Walk-coolers							
Ventilation Grills							
Etc....							

Staff members initial on the day they complete the task. On the daily tasks, they would initial on each day. On the weekly tasks, they would initial only on the day of the week they do that task.

Your notes:

Module 8

Managing Waste & Pest Control

The goal of this section is to understand the appropriate methods of hygienically collecting, storing and disposing of waste materials and how to properly control pests in a food facility.

Managing Waste

1 Goal

The goal of this section is to understand the appropriate methods of hygienically collecting, storing and disposing of waste materials.

Things to Remember

Waste not collected can:

- Makes cleaning difficult

- Allow for pest infestation

- Cross-contaminate food and food contact surfaces

Important Messages on Managing Waste

- Use storage bins that are easily identifiable as waste bins and cannot be mistaken for food containers.

- Typically, food containers are white, but garbage bins are dark with black garbage bags.

- Have enough tight waterproof waste bins in food preparation areas. This will prevent waste from overflowing and contaminating floors and food equipment.

- Empty internal waste bins often.

- Ensure that waste bins are cleaned and washed during with the cleaning schedule.

- External waste bins need to have a lid or a cover to keep pests away and prevent an infestation. The area should also be kept clean and free of garbage and other debris.

- Remember to wash your hands after handling garbage bags, or containers

Sewage and Other Liquid Waste

- Liquid was can contain pathogens and cross contaminate food. For example, the pathogen Listeria Monocytogenes was detected in food facility drain effluents.

- Sewage water systems have to be flushed out on a regular basis as part of a routine maintenance schedule.

Your notes:

Pest Control

 Goal

The goal of this section is to understand the conditions those attract pests and prevent pests from entering the food facility.

Things to Remember

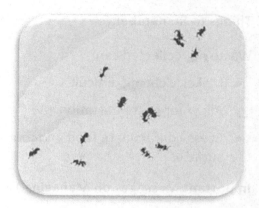

- Pests such as mice, flies, cockroaches and beetles can carry harmful microbes and will contaminate the food and food surfaces that they come in contact.

- The presence of one of those pests can lead to a severe infestation if not prevented and treated appropriately.

Controlling Pests in a Food Facility

Pest management is about prevention!

Once an infestation occurs, it is difficult to eliminate without the use of pesticide chemicals.

> *Only a licensed pest control professional should apply pesticide in a food facility. No insecticides or other poisons can be stored in a food facility. This includes over the counter pesticides like RAID.*

Important Steps in an Integrated (Preventative) Pest Management Program:
1. Keep pests out!

    a. You can do this by making sure your outside doors and windows are tight fitting, never left open without a screen, and are in good repair.

    b. Any gaps or holes leading to the outside are filled in and repaired immediately.

2. Clean, Clean, Clean!

    a. Regular cleaning removes any "food" for the pests and reduces the chances of an infestation.

    b. Clean as you go and stick to a regular cleaning schedule.

3. Store foods (especially dry goods) in closed tight fitting food-grade containers.

4. Watch for pest activity

    a. Check that there are no signs of pests such as insect trails or mouse droppings.

    b. Regularly check (or ensure that your pest control operator checks) the bait stations.

5. Follow the recommendations of your pest control operator.

Your notes:

HACCP

The goal of this section is to understand what the acronym HACCP stands for, how it works, and why it is widely used as a food safety management system in the food industry.

Hazard Analysis Critical Control Point (HACCP)

1   Goal

The goal of this section is to understand what the acronym HACCP stands for, how it works, and why it is widely used as a food safety management system in the food industry.

What is HACCP?

HACCP is a food safety system that identifies and controls food safety hazards to prevent foodborne illness.

This system was first developed in the 1960's, by the Pillsbury Corporation with NASA to ensure food safety for the first manned space missions.

It later gained wide adoption - the World Health Organization states that: *"HACCP has become the universally recognized and accepted method for food safety assurance"*.
http://www.who.int/foodsafety/fs_management/haccp/en/

HACCP principles identify critical areas in a food business and put control measures in place.

However, before applying the HACCP principles, basic food safety programs (often referred to as Good Manufacturing Practices or GMPs) have to be in place.

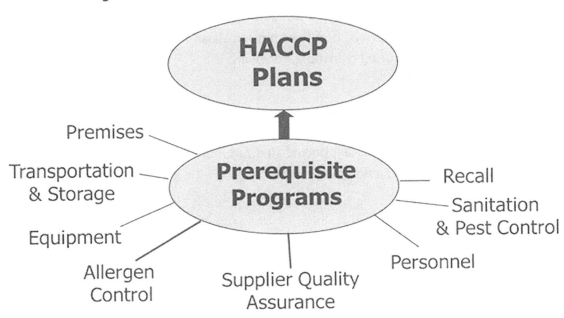

These GMPs are:

- Premises (Essentially the same as facility design and maintenance)
- Transportation and storage of food
- Equipment
- Allergen Control
- Supplier Quality Assurance
- Staff training
- Sanitation
- Pest Control
- Recall and traceability

Premises

- Controls Building maintenance and construction
- Manages outside Property (roadways, surroundings)
- Sanitary facilities
- Water / Steam / Ice Quality and Supply

Transportation and Storage

- Controls hazards of Food transportation and receiving
- Storage of incoming materials, non-food chemicals and finished product
- Temperature Control during transport, receiving

Equipment

- Design, construction, and installation of all equipment and utensils
- Equipment Maintenance and Calibration

Personnel Training

- General food hygiene training
- Technical training

Sanitation and Pest Control

- Cleaning and sanitizing of equipment and facilities
- Pre-operational inspection
- Pest Control Program

Important Note: In Alberta Regulation, a Cleaning Schedule and Pest Control documentation are required.

Recall

- Recall Procedures for bringing back food products after they have been distributed to the customer. The recall could be due to a hazard such as contamination with a pathogen or it could also be due to a labelling error.
- Distribution Records are required
- Methods of identification (lot #'s, codes, dates)
- Customer contacts information is documented
- Procedures are often to developed for what to do with an affected product
- Mock recalls are done routinely to make sure the process is working properly

Allergen Control

- Identifying the allergens in the facility and products produced
- Put in-plant control measures
- Putting the names of the allergens in the labelling and product packaging

In a traditional HACCP system, these GMPs are developed and documented. They control the majority of hazards in a food production facility.

There are many HACCP standards available in the industry. The Canadian Food Inspection Agency requires their food facilities to have a full HACCP system as part of their requirement for federally registered food facilities.

Once the GMPs have been fully developed, a food business can begin to implement the HACCP principles.

The Seven HACCP Principles are:

1. Conduct a Hazard Analysis
2. Determine Critical Control Points
3. Establish Critical Limits
4. Determine Procedures to Monitor the Critical Control Points
5. Establish Corrective Action
6. Establish procedures for Verification
7. Record Keeping

Explaining the steps of HACCP is best described using an example. Let's go through the HACCP steps in the simple example of cooking a hamburger.

Step #1. Conduct a Hazard Analysis

In this step we ask what are the hazards of our product – ground meat. Here are the hazards and how we can control them.

HAZARD	How it is controlled	What GMP can be used to control the hazard
Chemical contamination	- Only purchase food that is approved - Handle chemicals safely	- Supplier Quality Assurance - Sanitation program - Proper food storage
Physical contamination	- Only purchase food that is approved - Make sure food is not contaminated by equipment	- Supplier Quality Assurance - Equipment maintenance
Biological contamination	We can anticipate that raw ground meat is going to have pathogens such as E.Coli O157:H7.	We would need to make sure that it is cooked to internal temperature of 74°C **(165°F).**

Step #2: Determine Critical Control Points

In this step we identify the critical control point in the process. A critical control point (CCP) is an important part of the process designed to prevent or eliminate a hazard or reduce it to an acceptable level. It is also typically the last part of the production where that hazard can be controlled.

Here are some examples of CCPs may include:

- cooking
- metal detection

In the example mentioned above, our cooking step is the critical control point as it is the most critical step in killing pathogens to a safe level on the hamburger.

Step #3: Establish Critical Limits

In this step we identify the measurement that we need to have to make sure the critical control point is effective in controlling the hazard.

In the example above, our critical limit is the cooking temperature of the hamburger 74°C **(165°F).**

Step #4: Determine procedures to monitor the Critical Control Point

This steps asks how can we measure the critical control point process and make sure the critical limit is being achieved.

In the example above, the monitoring step is going to be taking the internal temperature of the hamburger with a probe thermometer.

Step #5: Establish Corrective Action

In this step, we say what we would do if the critical limit was not achieved.

In the example above, if the internal temperature of the hamburger did not reach 74°C (165°F) the corrective action could be to cook the food longer.

Step #6: Establish Procedures for Verification

In this steps, we build in a check system to make sure the process is happening appropriately.

In the example above, the verification step could be for a manager or an owner to check that the staff are following the correct cooking procedure.

Step #7: Record Keeping

A large component of a traditional HACCP system is the record keeping or documentation of the various processes.

In our example above, the cook would record the temperature of the hamburger on a record form.

> **This complete HACCP system is often utilized in food manufacturing. Food Service and Food Retail operations modify this system to meet the unique needs of their work environment.**

Your notes:

Modifying HACCP for the Food Service Environment

Several aspects of the traditional HACCP system are difficult to apply in a food service environment and that's why it was modified to meet this unique environment.

The same concepts are still applied just in a different way than in a food manufacturing setting. The biggest way the program was modified is by reducing the required records and documentation in a food service setting.

In a food service setting, there are typically two types of documentation:

- Food Safety Procedures
- Record keeping

Food Safety Procedures:

They outline all food safety requirements making sure to cover all the important or critical aspects such as cooking, cooling, and other food safety topics.

The guidebook we provided you here in this can be used and modified to be a facility's food safety procedures.

Feel free to add your own menu items and other process that are not listed in the guidebook and make it your own.

You can use the guidebook and the food safety procedures to train new staff.

Here's an example Food Safety Procedure:

Goal: To ensure that hot food is handled properly and that temperature abuse does not occur.

Who: Everyone responsible for buffet set up and service

What: Use a thermometer to check the temperature of the food and make sure it is above 60°C/140°C. Record the temperature on the provided temperature log.

When: At the beginning of the buffet set up and periodically every hour.

What to do if something goes wrong: If the temperature is not at or above 60°C/140°C then remove the food immediately from buffet and discard it. Check that the machine is plugged in, the temperature dial gauge is set appropriately, and call supervisor before refilling it with fresh properly cooked food.

In the example above you can see how the principles of HACCP are used but in a simplified way.

Food Safety Procedure tips:

For critical points such as cooking, you may want to group like menu items when developing your procedures. For example, hamburger, chicken burgers or any other ground meat cooking will all have a similar procedure and similar safe internal temperature cooking requirements.

Managing your Food Safety System and Staff Training:

Remember that as owners, managers, and food handlers, food safety is everyone's responsibility in the food facility.

Formal training and on-going food safety training is a key part of a strong food safety system. Training is done formally and on the job.

Formal training: This is training that includes food safety materials taught by a qualified food safety expert. This course would qualify as formal training. On-going formal training is highly recommended.

In-house training: It is recommended that each food facility have a set of procedures and food safety information specific to their menu / food preparation practices. This can be used to train new staff. This combined with formal training programs can set up an employee for success as well as protect the consumer and the business from foodborne illness.

On-the job training: This is done as the employee starts work by "showing" and supervising the new employee while they handle food. Having a "mentor" or a more senior employee work with the new employee is an effective way to ensure good food safety habits are formed.

In order to make sure that all food handlers are knowledgeable in food safety, a refresher course and on-going training is highly recommended.

Another great way to keep food safety top of mind, post food safety information on bulletin boards and other regular work areas.

Managers and supervisors should also watch for unsafe staff habits and make sure they are changed to safe habits.

Finally, it is important for everyone to make sure that they and others around them are demonstrating good food safety processes.

Steps to Managing Food Safety in a Food Service Environment:

Step #1: Ensure that you and your staff have completed food safety training that meets Section 31 of the Alberta Food Regulation.

Step #2: Develop procedures for safe food handling in your facility. Procedures should be specific to your operation and your menu items.

Step #3: Have in-house food safety training program for new staff and for on-going training. This guidebook can be used to train new staff and for on-going training for existing staff.

Step #4: Monitor/supervise staff to ensure they are building good food safety habits.

Step #5: Look for ways to improve food safety in your facility. Food Safety is an on-going effort and owners/managers should be on the look-out for ways to improve food safety in their facility.

Final Note:

Hi Everyone, Michael here. I want to leave you with a parting thought – I firmly believe that food safety is one of the most important systems in any food business and should be deliberately designed and actively managed.

The best way to create a food safety system in your business is through a combination of documenting your food safety processes and on-going staff training.

We have created a fantastic way to make sure your staff are constantly exposed to safe food handling procedures. If you want to learn about our on-going training program, contact me directly – michael@leanrhino.com

Thanks very much!

Michael

Made in the USA
Columbia, SC
20 January 2018